RECORDED VERSIONS GUITAR

AUTHENTIC TRANSCRIPTIONS
WITH NOTES AND TABLATURE

Transcribed By
ANDY ROBYNS

BON JO

Photography: Anton Corbijn and Mark Weiss

NOTICE
This publication is not authorised for sale in North America,
South America and Japan.

Unauthorised reproduction of any part of this publication by any means
including photocopying is an infringement of copyright.

Distributed by
MUSIC SALES LIMITED

Copyright © 1995 by Music Sales Limited
Order No. AM933273   ISBN 0-7119-5282-5
All Rights Reserved. International Copyright Secured.

Exclusive distributors:
Music Sales Limited, 8/9 Frith Street, London W1V 5TZ, United Kingdom.
Music Sales Pty Limited, 120 Rothschild Avenue, Rosebery, NSW 2018, Australia.

BON JOVI
CROSS ROAD

Livin' On A Prayer

Words and Music by Jon Bon Jovi, Richie Sambora and Desmond Child

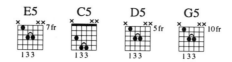

Intro

Moderate Rock ♩ = 122

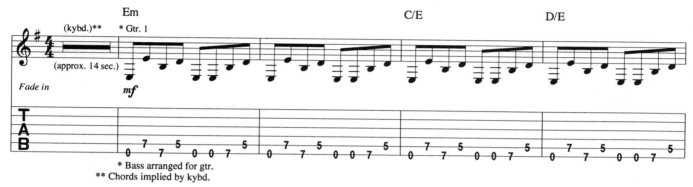

* Bass arranged for gtr.
** Chords implied by kybd.

Gtr. 1 cont. simile

Rhy. Fig. 1

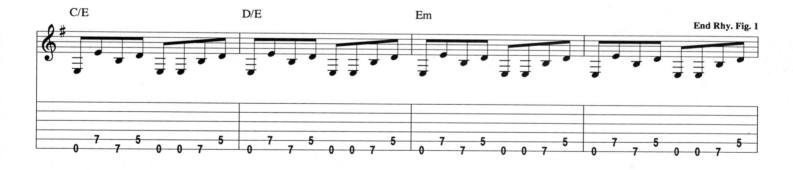

End Rhy. Fig. 1

Spoken: Once upon a time, not so long ago...

Verse

Gtr. 2 tacet, 1st time
Gtr. 2: w/ Rhy. Fig. 1, 2 times, 2nd time

(N.C.)Em

1. Tom-my used to work on the docks. ___ Un-ion's been on strike, he's down on his luck, it's
2. Tom-my's got his six string in hock. ___ Now he's hold-ing in when he used to make it talk so

Gtr. 3: w/ Fill 1, 2nd time

C5   D5   N.C.(Em)

tough, ___ so tough. ___ Gi-na works the din-er all day.
tough, ___ mmm, it's tough. ___ Gi-na dreams of run-ning a - way.

Gtr. 2

Work-ing for her man, she brings home her pay for love, ___ mmm, for love. ___
When she cries in the night, Tom-my whis-pers; "Ba-by, it's o - kay, ___ some -

C5   D5

Pre-Chorus

N.C.(Em)   C5 D5   E5   C5   D5

She says we've got to { hold on ___ to what we've got. It does-n't make a dif-f'rence if we
___ day." ___ We've got to {

* w/ out talk box.

Fill 1

8va -

Gtr. 3 (dist.)

w/ talk box   f   full   w/ bar
            full

full
14   14   (14)   (14)   20   (20)   15
                                              17   0

Keep The Faith

Words and Music by Jon Bon Jovi, Richie Sambora and Desmond Child

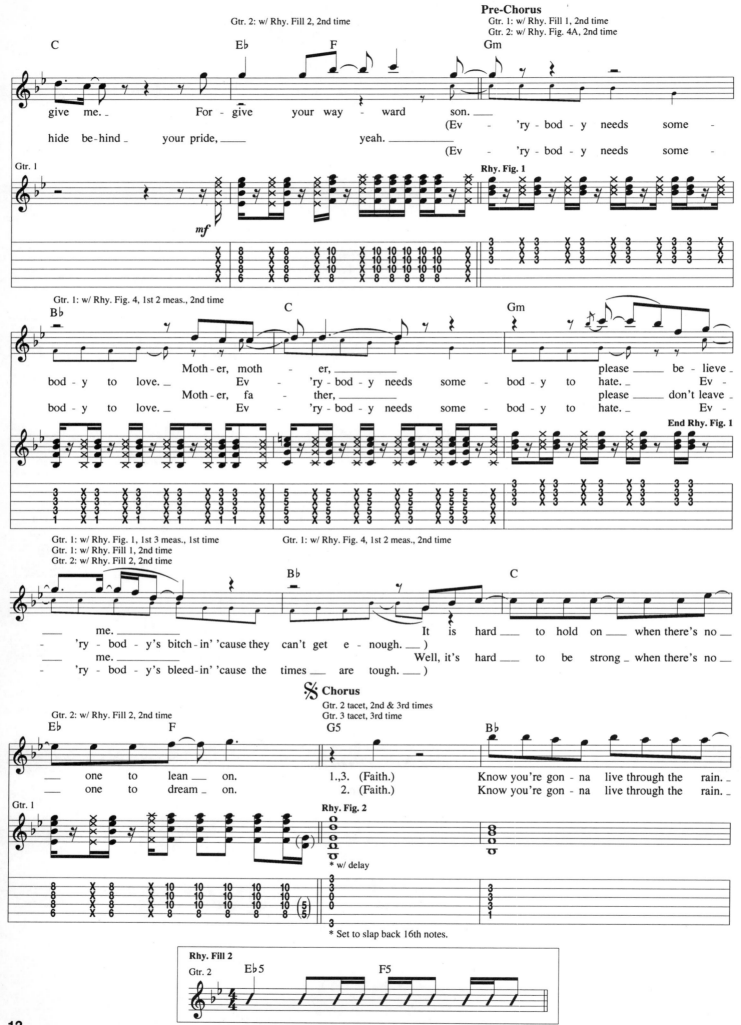

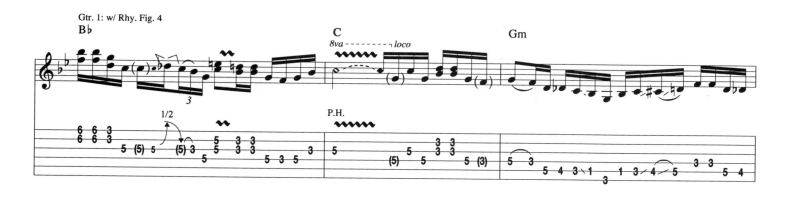

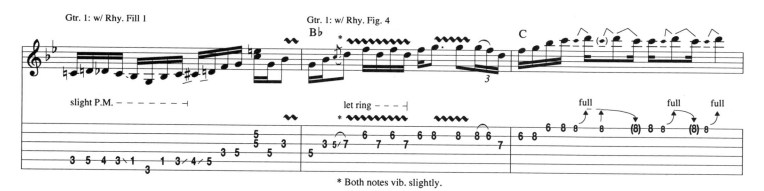

* Both notes vib. slightly.

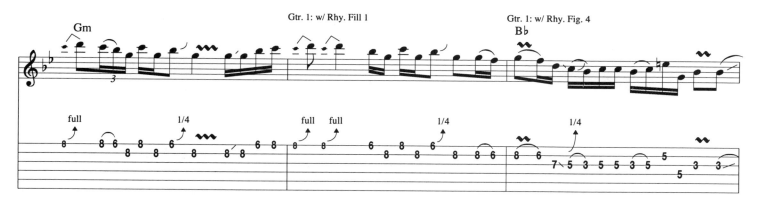

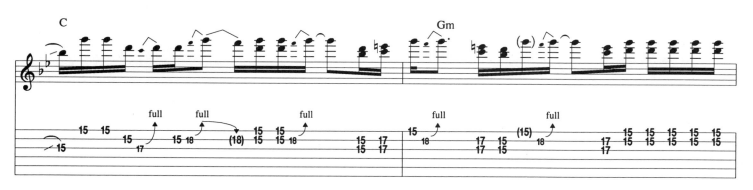

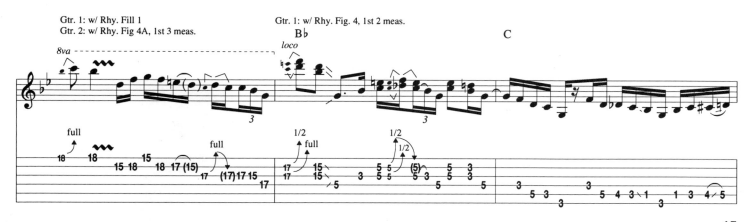

16

Someday I'll Be Saturday Night

Words and Music by Jon Bon Jovi,
Richie Sambora and Desmond Child

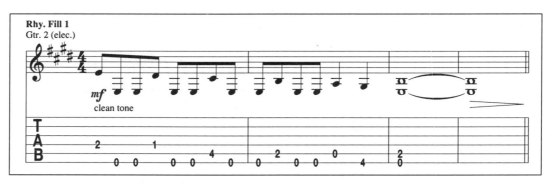

Thurs-days, Fri - days, ain't _ been kind. _ But some-how I've _ sur - vived. _

% Chorus

Hey, man, I'm a - live _ I'm tak - ing each day _ a night ____ at a time.

Yeah, I'm down, ___ but I know I'll _ get by. ___ Hey, hey, hey, hey _

*Two gtrs. arr. for one.

Fill 1
Gtr. 2

Fill 2
Gtr. 3 (acous.)
mp
w/ slide

Fill 4
Gtr. 4

Fill 5
Gtr. 3
w/ slide

Fill 7
Gtr. 3
w/ slide

Guitar Solo

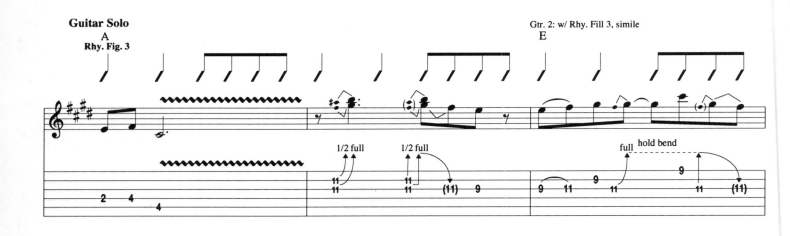

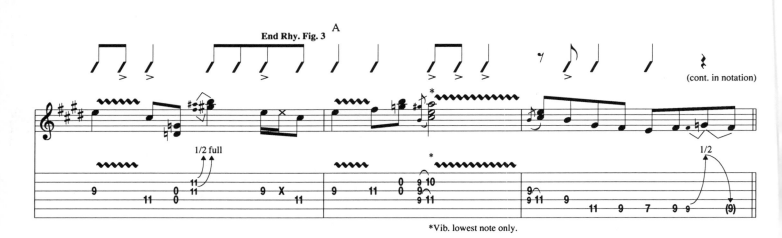

*Vib. lowest note only.

Bridge

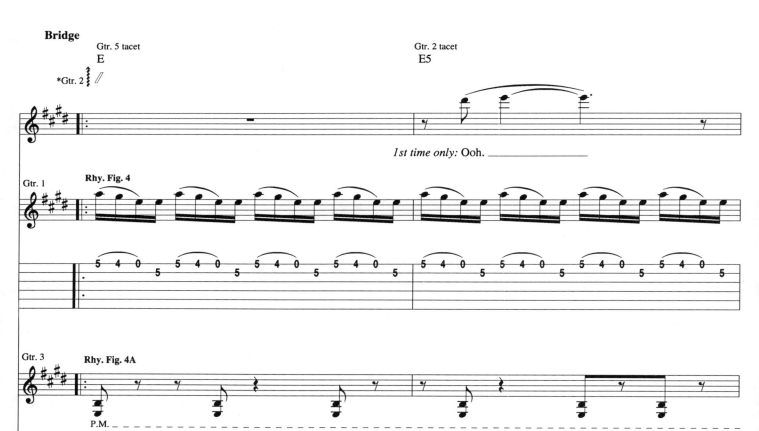

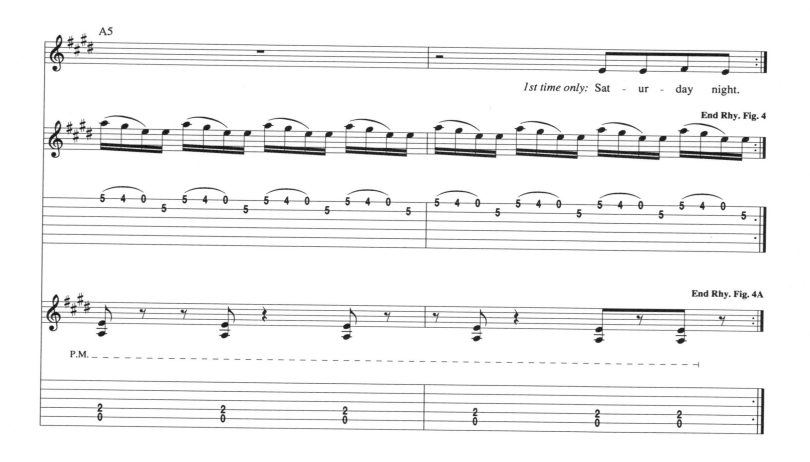

1st time only: Sat - ur - day night.

End Rhy. Fig. 4

End Rhy. Fig. 4A

P.M. —

Gtrs. 1 & 3: w/ Rhy. Figs. 4 & 4A, 2 times

E5   A5

Some - day I'll be Sat - ur - day night. __ I'll be back on my feet. I'll be do - ing al - right. It

Gtr. 6 (acous.)

f

w/ slide —

full

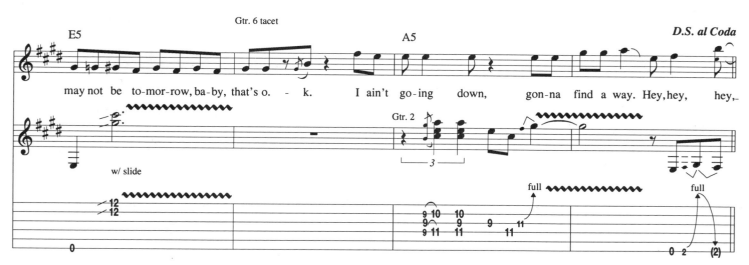

Gtr. 6 tacet

E5   A5   *D.S. al Coda*

may not be to - mor - row, ba - by, that's o. - k. I ain't go - ing down, gon - na find a way. Hey, hey, hey, —

Gtr. 2

w/ slide

full

full

23

⊕ Coda

Gtr. 2: w/ Rhy. Fill 3, 1st 2 meas.

Gtr. 2: w/ Rhy. Fill 5

Gtr. 1

Gtr. 5

night. Oh. I'm feel-ing like a Mon-day, but some-

Gtr. 2: w/ Rhy. Fill 3, 5 times

day I'll be Sat-ur-day night.

Outro

Gtr. 1: w/ Rhy. Fig. 3, 4 1/2 times, simile

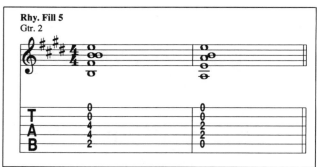

Rhy. Fill 5
Gtr. 2

24

Always

Words and Music by Jon Bon Jovi

say your prayers try to un-der-stand, I've made mis-takes, I'm just a man. When he

holds _ you close, when he pulls you near, when he says the words _ you've been mean-ing to hear. I wish

I was him with those words of mine, _ just to say _ to you till the end of time. And _

I will love _ you, _ ba - by, al - ways. And I'll _

*Gtr. 2 right of slash in TAB.

Pre-Chorus

𝄋 Chorus

Rhy. Fig. 2

Well, there
ain't no luck in these load-ed dice. _ But ba-by, if you give me just one more try, _ we could
pack up our old dreams and our old lives. We'll find a place where the sun still shines. Yeah, _
I'll be there _ till the stars _ don't shine, till the heav-ens burst and the words don't rhyme. I know

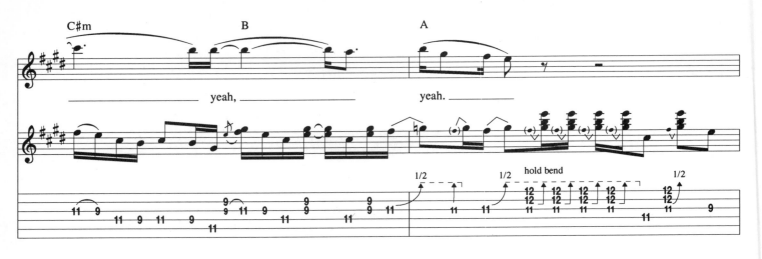

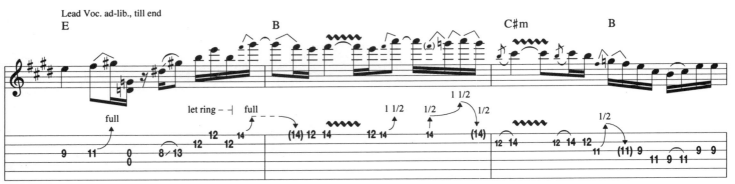

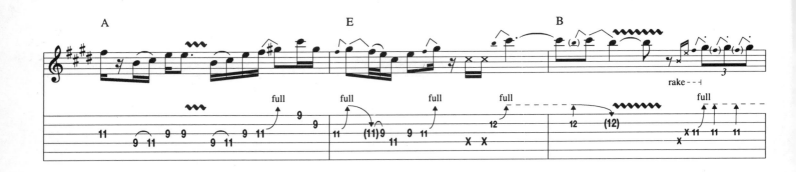

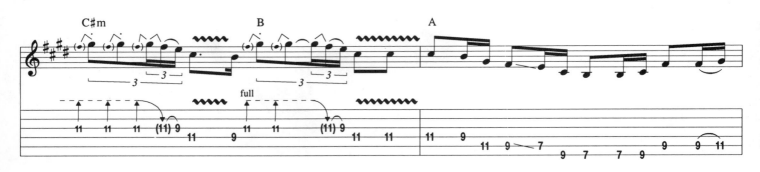

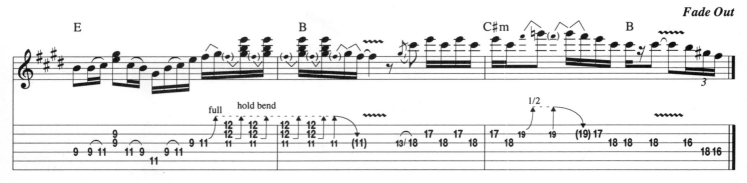

Wanted Dead Or Alive

Words and Music by Jon Bon Jovi and Richie Sambora

*Play 3rd time only.
**Play simile 2nd & 3rd times.

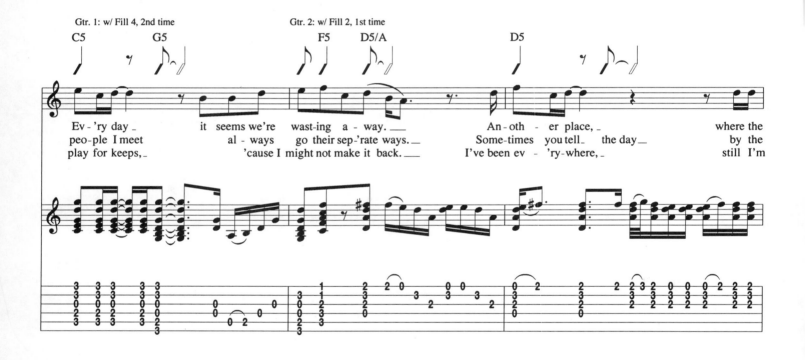

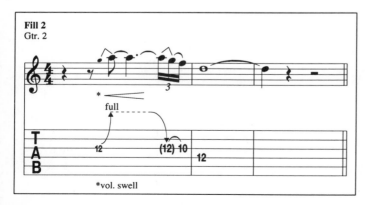

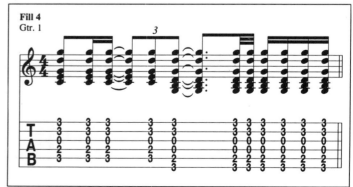

Chorus

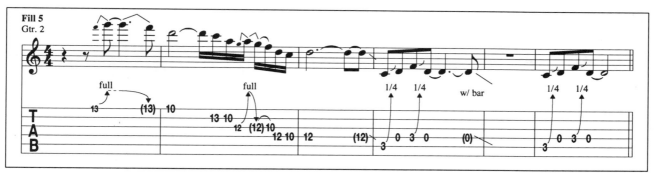

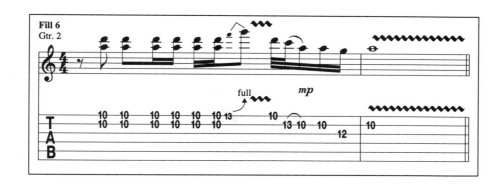

⊕ Coda

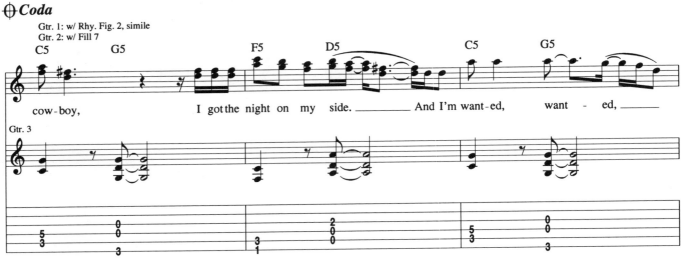

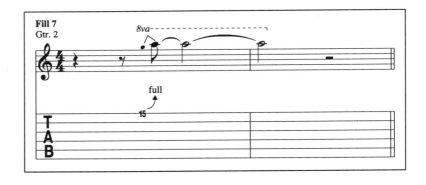

drive, __ I still drive, _____ dead or a - live, __ dead or a - live, _____

dead or a - live, __ dead or a - live, _____ dead or a - live. _____

Outro

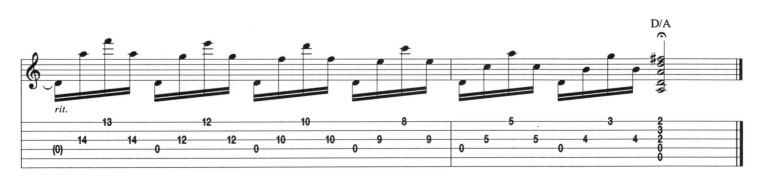

Lay Your Hands On Me

Words and Music by Jon Bon Jovi and Richie Sambora

1. If you're read - y, I'm will - ing and a - ble. Help me

lay my ___ cards out on the ta - ble.

You're mine ___ and I'm yours for the tak -

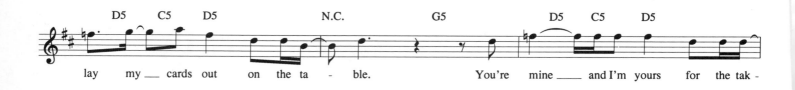

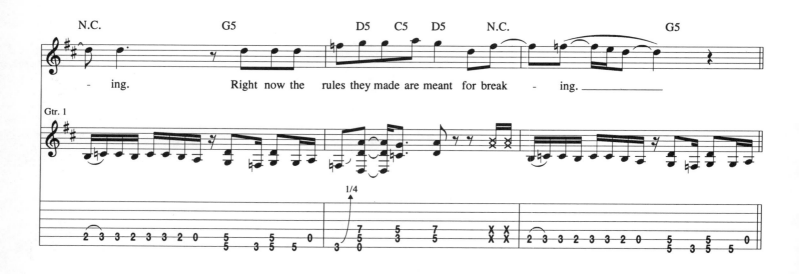

- ing.   Right now the   rules they made are meant for break   - ing. _____

𝄋 Pre-Chorus

1. What you get ain't al - ways what you see. ___   But sat - is - fac - tion is   guar - an - teed.   They   say
2. Ev - ry thing you want is what I need. ___   Your sat - is - fac - tion is   guar - an - teed.   But   the

Verse

Gtr. 1: w/ Rhy. Fill 1   Gtr. 1: w/ Rhy. Fig. 1, 1 1/2 times, simile

D5 C5 D5   N.C.   G5   D5 C5 D5   N.C.   G5

-er,   I'm a po-et,   I'm a preach-er.   I've been to school, _ and ba-by, I've been the teach - er._____ If you

D.S. al Coda

D5 C5 D5   N.C.   G5   D5   C5   D5   N.C.   G5

show me how to get up off _ the ground _ right now,   I can show you how _ to fly   and nev-er ev-er come _ back down._

Gtr. 1

⊕ *Coda*

D5 C D5   **Guitar Solo**   D5 Cadd9 D5/A

Gtr. 1

*Gtr. 2 (dist.)

fdbk.   rake
1/2

* Standard Tuning

D5 Cadd9 D5   D5 Cadd9 D5

w/ bar   -1 1/2   1/2   1/2

-1 1/2

44

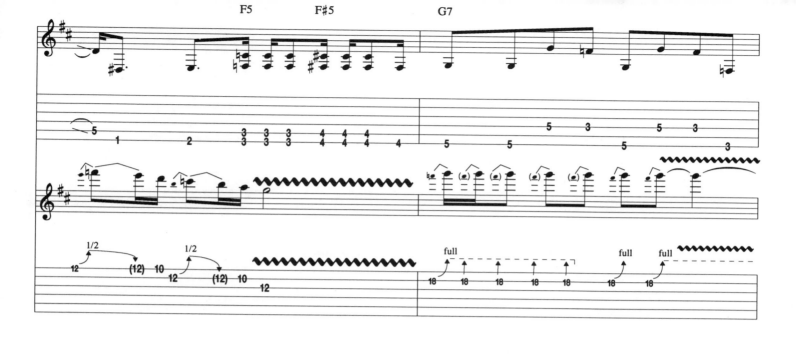

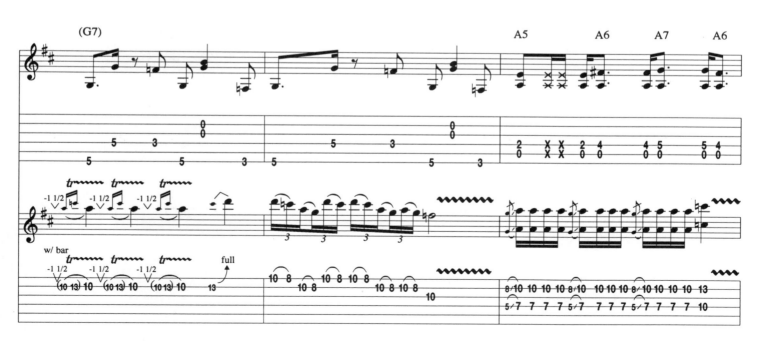

Pre-Chorus

Oh, whoa, whoa, ba-by, don't you know I on-ly aim to please. ___

If ___ you want me to lay my hands on ___ you. _____ Whoa,

oh. ____ What-cha got-ta do ___ is ___ lay 'em on me. Well, come on, come on, come

* Chords implied by kybd.

on. And Ev-'ry-bod-y's gon-na help me now. ___ I can feel the peo-ple sing. I can feel my

Bkgd. Voc. Fig. 1

Lay ___ your hands on ___ me, lay ___ your hands on ___ me, lay ___ your hands on ___ me. ____

You Give Love A Bad Name

Words and Music by Jon Bon Jovi, Richie Sambora and Desmond Child

Verse

Gtr. 1: w/ Rhy. Fig. 1, 4 times

N.C. (Cm)

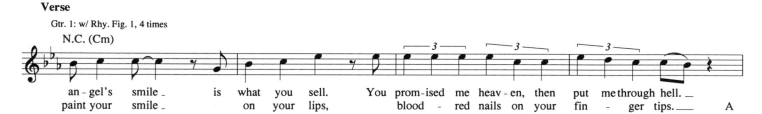

an - gel's smile _ is what you sell. You prom-ised me heav - en, then put me through hell. _
paint your smile _ on your lips, blood - red nails on your fin - ger tips. _ A

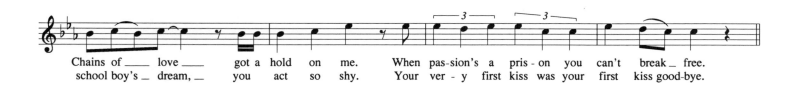

Chains of ___ love ___ got a hold on me. When pas-sion's a pris - on you can't break _ free.
school boy's _ dream, _ you act so shy. Your ver - y first kiss was your first kiss good-bye.

Pre-Chorus

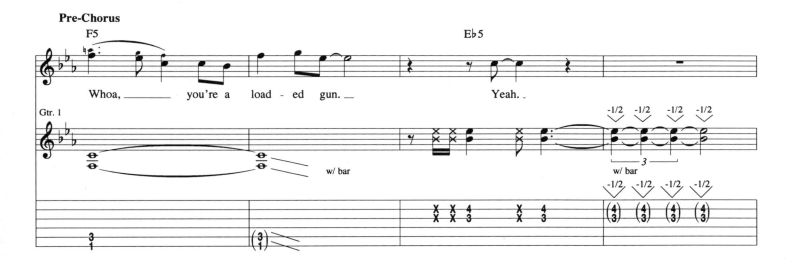

Whoa, _____ you're a load - ed gun. _ Yeah. _

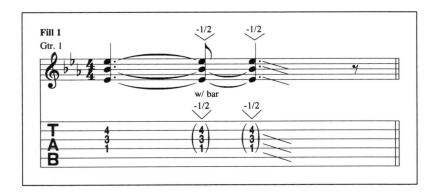

51

Shot through the heart, __ and you're to __ blame. You give love _____ a bad name, bad name. I

Gtr. 1

play my part, __ and you play your __ game. You give love _____ a bad name, bad name.

Outro *Play 3 Times and Fade*

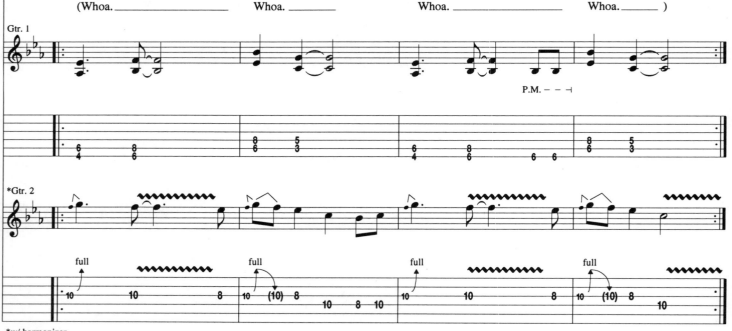

You give love. _____   You give love. ____   Bad name.
(Whoa._____   Whoa. _____   Whoa. _____   Whoa. _____)

Gtr. 1

P.M. — — ┤

*Gtr. 2

full   full   full   full

*w/ harmonizer

Bed of Roses

Words and Music by Jon Bon Jovi

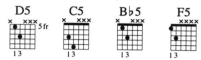

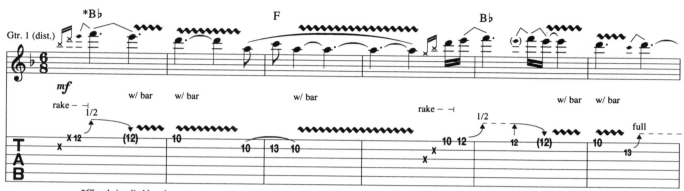

*Chords implied by piano.

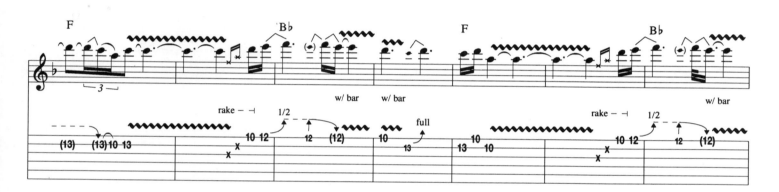

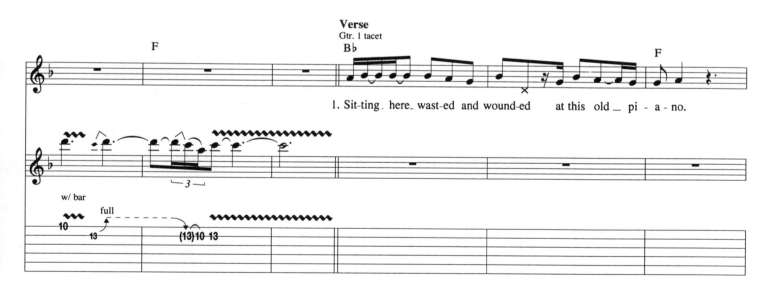

1. Sit-ting here wast-ed and wound-ed at this old pi-a-no.

Try-ing hard to cap-ture the mo-ment this morn-ing I don't know. 'Cause a

While some march-ing band keeps its own __ beat in my __ head while we're
A king's ran-som in dimes, I'd give each night to see through this

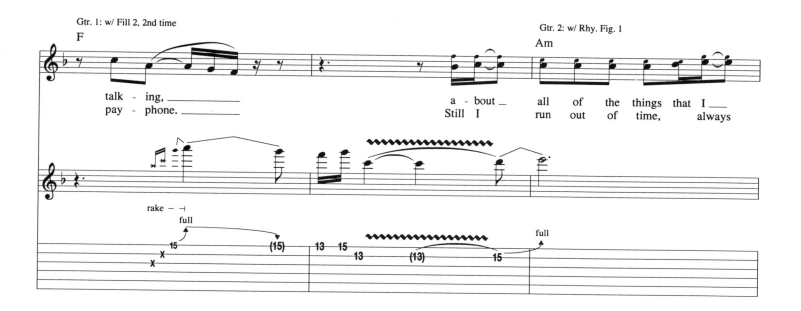

Gtr. 1: w/ Fill 2, 2nd time
F

Gtr. 2: w/ Rhy. Fig. 1
Am

talk - ing, _____
pay - phone. _____

a - bout __ all of the things that I __
Still I run out of time, always

rake
full
full

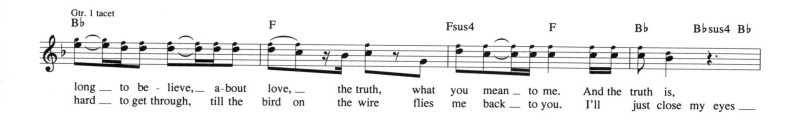

Gtr. 1 tacet
Bb   F   Fsus4   F   Bb   Bbsus4 Bb

long __ to be - lieve, __ a-bout love, __ the truth, what you mean __ to me. And the truth is,
hard __ to get through, till the bird on the wire flies me back __ to you. I'll just close my eyes __

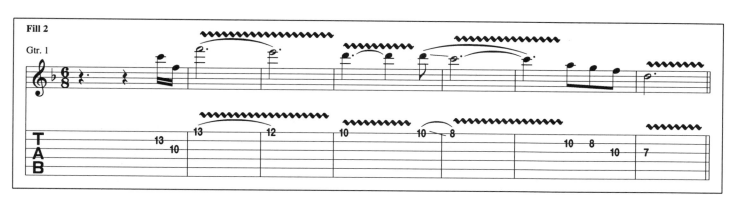

Fill 2

Gtr. 1

died. Ooh, yeah.

you close your eyes, _ know I'll be think-ing a - bout you. While _ my mis-tress, she calls _ me to

stand in her spot-light ___ a-gain. To-night I won't be a-lone, ___ but you know that don't mean I'm not

D.S. al Coda 1

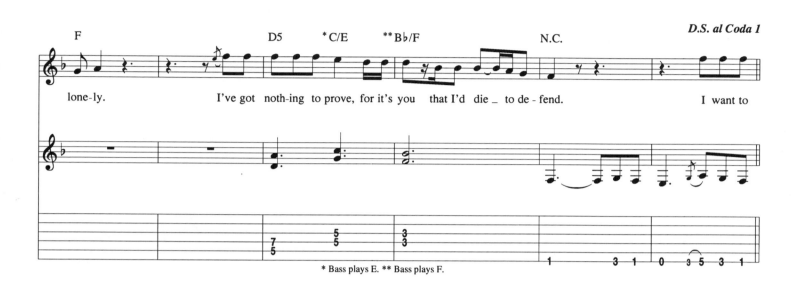

lone-ly. I've got noth-ing to prove, for it's you that I'd die _ to de-fend. I want to

* Bass plays E. ** Bass plays F.

⊕ Coda 1

D.S. al Coda 2

lay you ___ down. I want to

*Gtr. 3 only

⊕ Coda 2

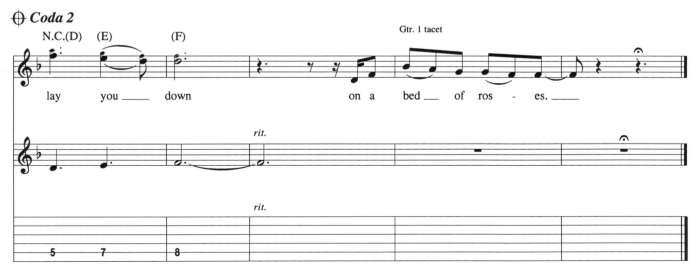

lay you ___ down on a bed ___ of ros - es. ___

Blaze Of Glory

Words and Music by Jon Bon Jovi

Verse
Gtrs. 1 & 2 tacet

D
④ open

Dm
Gtr. 4
(acous.)
mp

C

2. When you're brought in - to this world, ___   they
          ask a - bout my con - sience,   and I

Gtr. 2: w/ Fill 1, 2nd time

Em   G

Dm

say you're born in sin. ___   Well, at least   they gave me some - thing,   I did - n't have to
of - fer you my soul. ___   You ask if I'll grow to be ___ a wise ___ man,   ask   if I'll

Dm

Gtr. 2: w/ Fill 2, 2nd time

F

steal, ___ or have ___ to win.   Well, they   tell   me that ___ I'm want - ed, ___   yeah,
grow   old.   You   ask   me if ___ I've known love, and   what it's like to

C

G

I'm   a want - ed man. ___   I'm   a   colt   in your sta - ble, I'm what Cain   was to A - ble, mis - ter,
sing songs   in the rain. ___   Well, I've seen love come,   I've   seen   it shot down,   I've

Fill 1
Gtr. 2

w/ slide

Fill 2
Gtr. 2

w/ slide

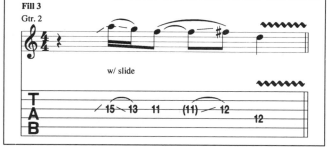

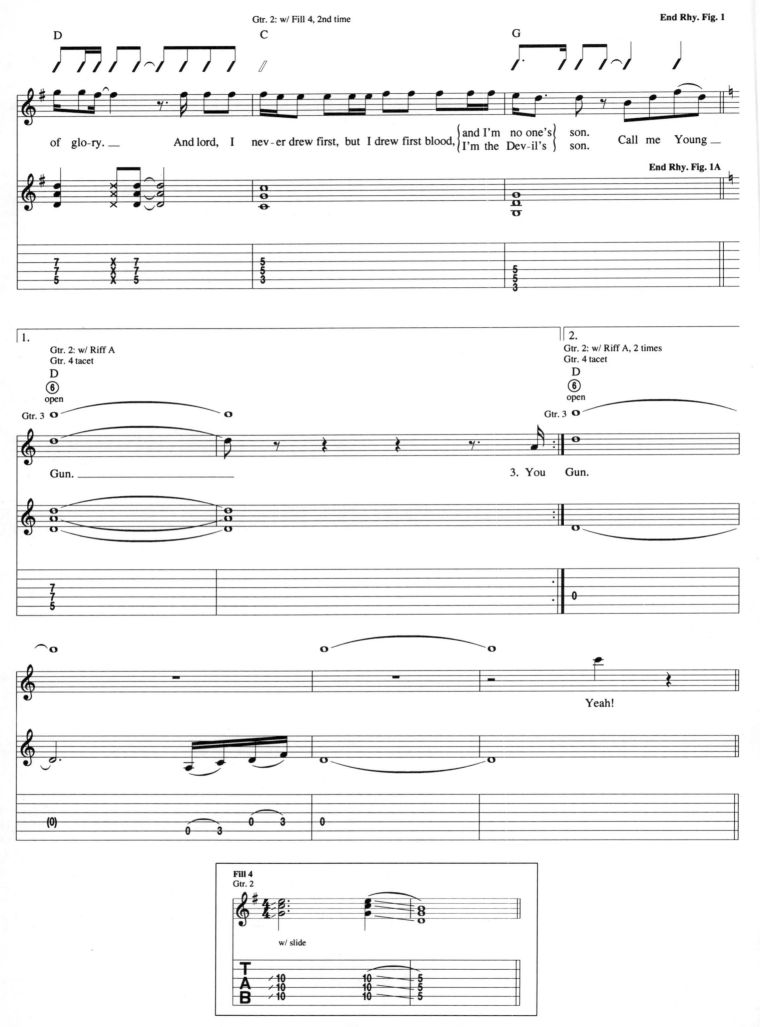

Guitar Solo

Verse

Gtrs. 2 & 5 tacet

4. Each night I go to bed, I pray the Lord my soul to keep. _ No, I ain't look-ing for for-give-ness, but be-

*Chords implied by kybd.

fore I'm six feet deep. Lord, _ I got to ask a fa - vor, and I hope you'll un-der-stand. _ 'Cause, I've

lived life to the ful-lest, let this boy _ die like a man. Star-ing down a bul-let, let me make_ my fi - nal _ stand.

Chorus

Gtr. 4 & 5: w/ Rhy. Figs. 1 & 1A

Shot down _ in a blaze of glo - ry. Take me now, ___ but know the truth. _ I'm go-ing

Gtr. 2

w/ slide

out ___ in a blaze of glo-ry. _ Lord, I nev-er drew first, but I drew first blood, and I'm no one's son._ Call me Young

Prayer '94

Words and Music by Jon Bon Jovi, Richie Sambora and Desmond Child

Bad Medicine

Words and Music by Jon Bon Jovi, Richie Sambora and Desmond Child

Bridge

I need a res-pi-ra-tor 'cause I'm run-ning out of breath or you're an

all night gen-er-a-tor wrapped in stock-ings and a dress. When you find your med-i-cine you'll

*Synth. arr. for gtr.

Fill 1

*Dive & vib. simultaneously.

take what you can get. 'Cause if there's some-thing bet-ter ba-by, well, they hav-'n't found it yet. Whoa, _____

Chorus
Gtr. 1: w/ Rhy. Fig. 1, 1st 7 meas.
* Gtr. 1: w/ Rhy. Fill 1, 2nd time

your love _ is like bad med-i-cine. Bad med-i-cine is what I _____ need. Whoa, _____

* Gtr. 1 plays Fill 1, then continues in Rhy. Fig. 1.

shake it up _____ just like bad med-i-cine. There ain't no doc-tor that can
2nd time: Your love's a po-tion that can

1.
cure my dis-ease. _

2.
Gtr. 1: w/ Rhy. Fig. 3
cure my dis-ease. _ Bad, bad med-i-cine _____ is

Gtr. 1   Rhy. Fill 2   End Rhy. Fill 2
let ring   (cont. in Rhy. Fill 1)   let ring

Gtr. 1: w/ Rhy. Fig. 3
what I want. _ Bad, bad med-i-cine. Oo, ba-by, oo, babe.

w/ bar

Rhy. Fill 1
Gtr. 1

77

I'll Be There For You

Words and Music by Jon Bon Jovi and Richie Sambora

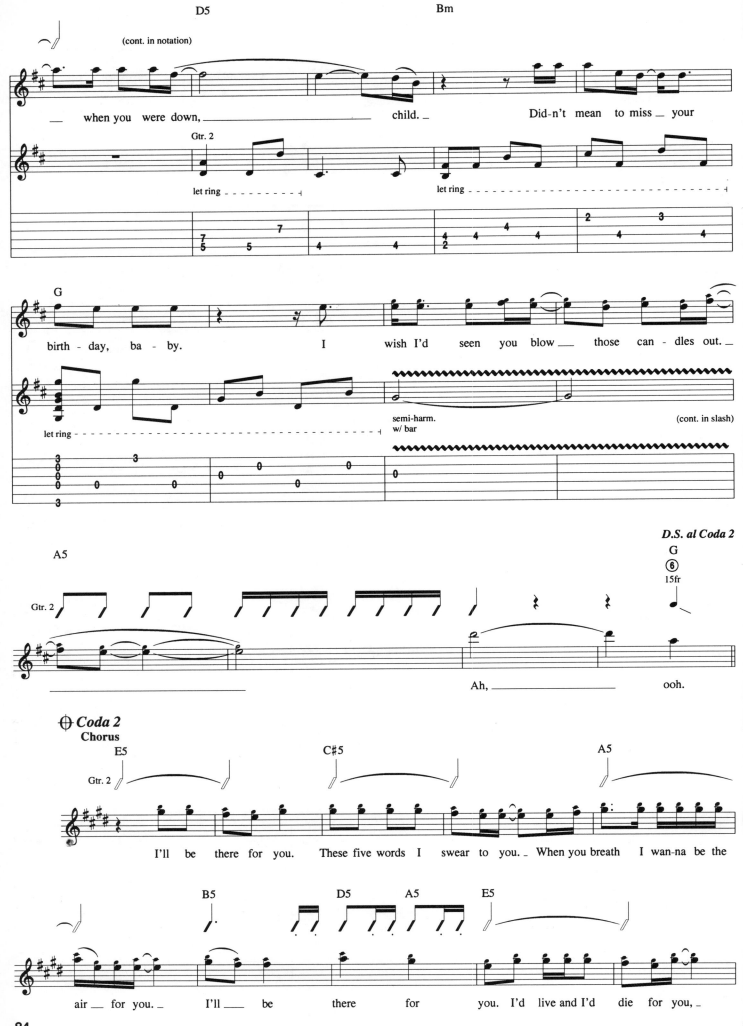

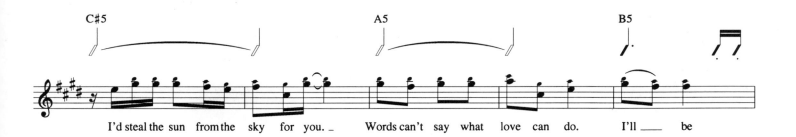

I'd steal the sun from the sky for you. __ Words can't say what love can do. I'll __ be

there for you. ____ *(Whoa. _____)

Whoa. _____

*2nd time only.

Whoa.

*rit.

*rit.   *(cont. in slash)

*2nd time only.

Outro

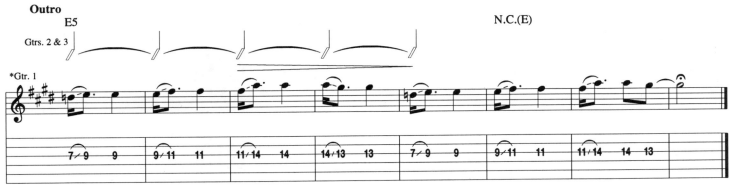

*Doubled w/ sitar.

In And Out Of Love

Words and Music by Jon Bon Jovi

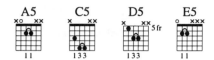

A5   C5   D5   E5

Intro
Moderate Rock ♩ = 128

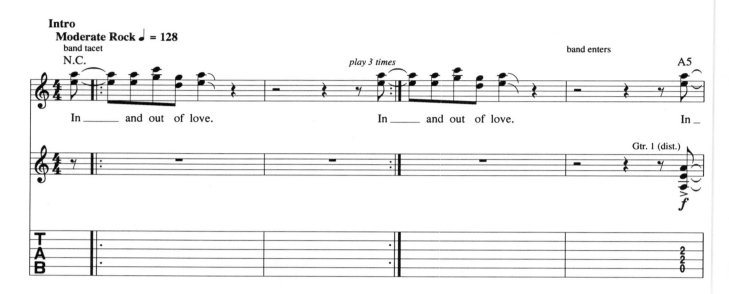

In _____ and out of love.   In _____ and out of love.   In

_____ and out of love.   In _____ and out of love.   1. You're a wi-

Verse

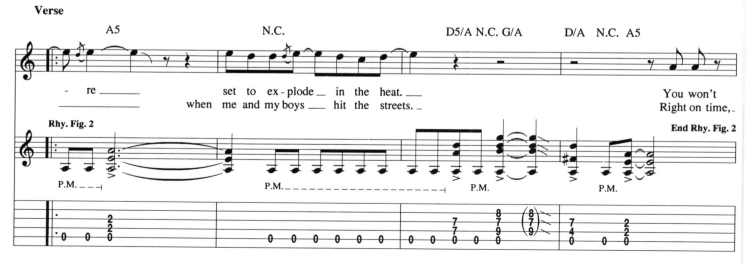

-re _____ set to ex-plode _____ in the heat. _____   You won't
when me and my boys _____ hit the streets. _____   Right on time,

Runaway

Words and Music by Jon Bon Jovi and George Karakoglou

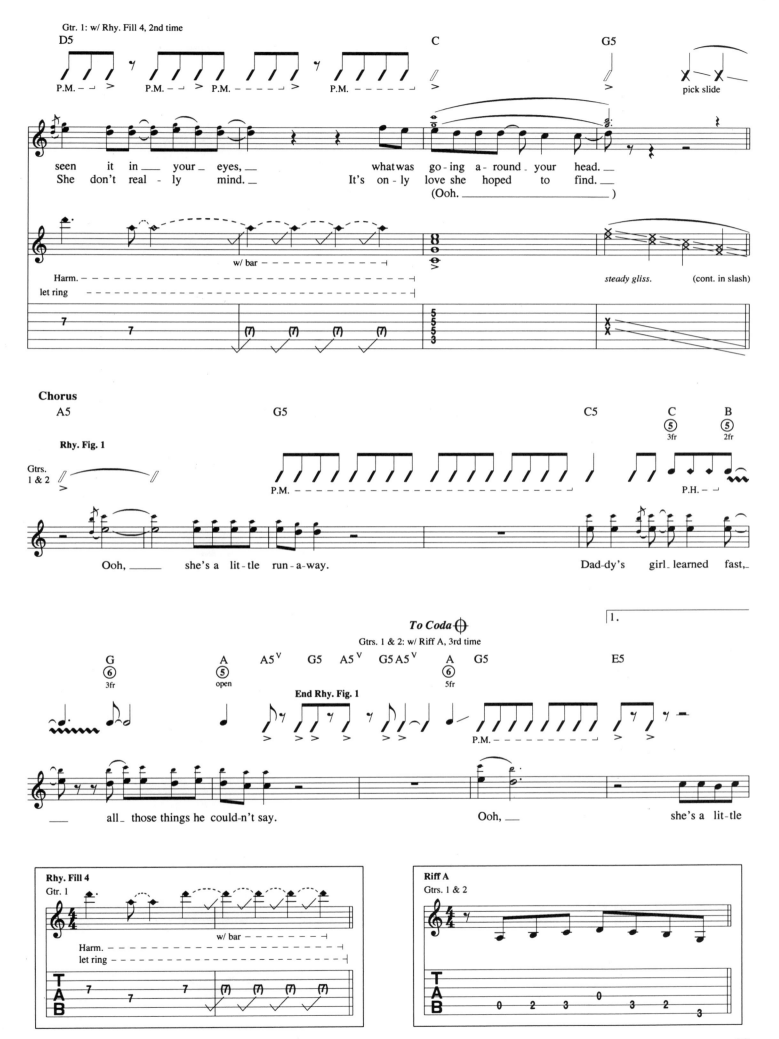

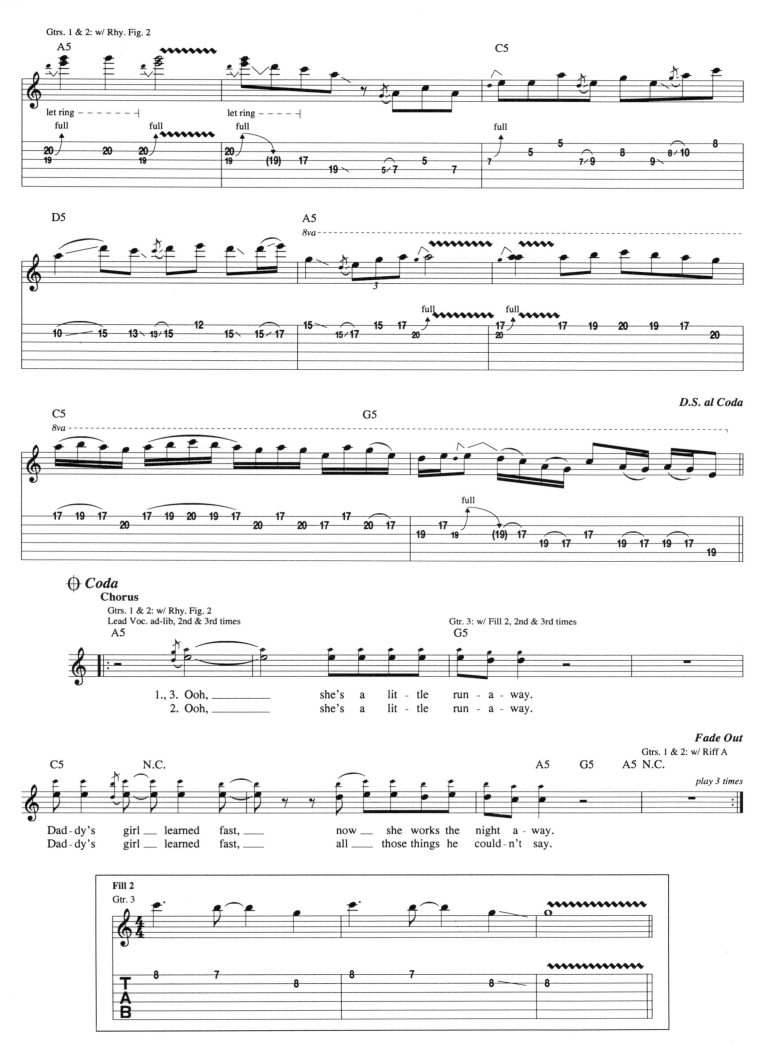

Gtrs. 1 & 2: w/ Rhy. Fig. 2

1., 3. Ooh, _____ she's a lit - tle run - a - way.
2. Ooh, _____ she's a lit - tle run - a - way.

Dad - dy's girl _ learned fast, ___ now _ she works the night a - way.
Dad - dy's girl _ learned fast, ___ all _ those things he could - n't say.

NOTATION LEGEND

Printed and bound in Great Britain by
Caligraving Limited Thetford Norfolk

5/01 (40204)